Children's Rules
for Parents

Children's Rules for Parents

Collected and Edited by

Michael Laser

and

Ken Goldner

Illustrated by Irene Trivas

PERENNIAL LIBRARY

Harper & Row, Publishers, New York
Cambridge, Philadelphia, San Francisco, Washington
London, Mexico City, São Paulo, Singapore, Sydney

CHILDREN'S RULES FOR PARENTS. Copyright © 1987 by Michael Laser and Ken Goldner. Illustrations copyright © 1987 by Irene Trivas. All rights reserved. Printed in the United States of America. No part of this book may be used or reproduced in any manner whatsoever without written permission except in the case of brief quotations embodied in critical articles and reviews. For information address Harper & Row, Publishers, Inc., 10 East 53rd Street, New York, N.Y. 10022. Published simultaneously in Canada by Fitzhenry & Whiteside Limited, Toronto.

FIRST EDITION

Designer: Erich Hobbing

Library of Congress Cataloging-in-Publication Data

Children's rules for parents.

1. Children—United States—Attitudes.
2. Parent and child—United States.   I. Laser,
Michael.   II. Goldner, Ken.
HQ772.5.C45   1987   305.2'3'0973   86-46078
ISBN 0-06-096173-2 (pbk.)

89   90   91   MPC   10   9   8   7   6   5   4   3

Contents

Other Issues

Foreword

Granted, being a good parent is one of the hardest jobs in the world.

Still, as ex-children, every one of us can remember certain things our parents did that—to put it gently —*we wish they hadn't*. Even the best parents make mistakes.

Adults think they remember all the pangs and injuries of childhood, but memories dim. The real experts on childhood's discontents are the people who are children now. That's why we went to them for their views on parenting. They may not be objective, but, like the patient in the doctor's office, the child is the one who knows where it hurts.

To reach all different kinds of children, we placed notices in two teachers' magazines, *NEA Today* and *Early Years*. We asked teachers to assign their first-through ninth-grade students to write rules for their parents and send the results to us. Then we sat back and waited to see what the mail would bring. Would the writing be funny or angry, heartwarming or profound?

The answer, as it turned out, was "All of the above." The book includes everything from playful wit to angry complaints, from unintentional knee-slappers to gentle pleas for what's only fair. Many of the entries describe the authors' visions of Paradise—

huge allowances, no vegetables or siblings, etc.—but others pinpoint wise and subtle truths. Often during the reading of the mail, I winced in recognition: *My parents did that too. How could I have forgotten?*

Much of the material is here simply because it's funny, but throughout parents will find reasonable complaints that should make them stop and think. If children had their way, I believe mothers and fathers would be required to read this book at least once a year, as a refresher course in parenting.

Some of these entries express ideas that appeared in *many* submissions. In cases where one wasn't clearly the best, we simply credited the student whose work arrived first.

We have corrected spelling except where the mistakes seemed to add to the charm.

The towns listed beneath the writers' names are the towns where their schools are located.

By Way of Introduction . . .

I feel it is not fair for parents to make all the rules. I would like to make some rules for them.

> Tomasina Clark, 6th Grade
> Bronx, New York

Be honest, how many of you adults actually understand the kids of today? I don't believe too many hands are up, and those that are shouldn't be.

> Steven C. Warren, 9th Grade
> Knoxville, Tennessee

In this day and age, kids have to have dominance over their parents.

> Marc Fioravanti, 8th Grade
> North Brunswick, New Jersey

Parents are a group of people known for their tendencies to be stubborn and overbearing. These rules should be used to train parents into the type of parents children could be proud of. Kind, considerate, and lovable are the adjectives used to describe children. Why can't parents be more like them?

> Felicia Rosenzweig, 8th Grade
> North Brunswick, New Jersey

1

Utopia!

I get to rule the house.

> Ryan Miller, 5th Grade
> Canton, Michigan

I get three of everything.

> Heather A. Zampardi, 6th Grade
> New Hartford, New York

Dads should say yes if mothers say no.

> Nicole Thompson, 3rd Grade
> Northridge, California

I wish they would be the children and we could be the parents and we could be the boss.

> Tiffanee Westland, 3rd Grade
> Northridge, California

Let me paint my room camouflage. Let me boobie trap my room. Get rid of the Sesame Street wallpaper, lamp and bedspread. Put an electric lock on my door, and I'm the only one who knows the combination.

> Ashton Smith
> Boiceville, New York

Let me watch the late and dirty shows. Drink beer on special occasions. Choose my own ways. Go to church when I want. Ride on the mud at the edge of the pond.

Gus Schnitzer
Boiceville, New York

I wish I could live with my boyfriend.

Andrea K. Gioulis, 3rd Grade
Northridge, California

My parents will soport me but I will be superior to them.

David Warner, 6th Grade
Glendale, Arizona

Parents should always drop their children at the entrance and then go find a place to park the car.

Heather Aldrich, 8th Grade
North Brunswick, New Jersey

On Saturday morning, the Smurfs are on,
So, parents, don't make your kid mow the lawn.
Kids, while they are young, should have a fun time
    and celebrate,
They will soon grow old, and take up responsibilities,
    but for right now,
let them party and stay up late.

Caroline Kim & Rebecca Wolf, 6th Grade
Herndon, Virginia

Get me everything purple.

Amy Moline, 4th Grade
Carroll, Ohio

Let me write on my room walls.

Steve Stock, 4th Grade
Indianapolis, Indiana

Servants are a must! If you cannot afford them, you the parent will wait on your child hand and foot.

Tina Brostek, 6th Grade
Syracuse, New York

You can't leave to go to Bloomingdale's without me.

Olivia Kany, 5th Grade
Pelham, New York

Turning the Tables:
Revenge is Sweet

Parents should be seen and not heard.

Marc Fioravanti, 8th Grade
North Brunswick, New Jersey

Some parents should be seen and not heard, others shouldn't even be seen.

Rachel Anne Baiera, 6th Grade
Deer Park, New York

They make us suffer. We should make them suffer.

Denise Wenzel
Junction City, Wisconsin

My mom and dad cannot talk at the supper table.

Laurie Beiter, 4th Grade
Carroll, Ohio

When a parent is unfair to you, it doesn't mean you have to be unfair, but you can get even in a nice syvilized way.

Frank Caridi, 6th Grade
Burr Ridge, Illinois

Don't allow your parents to have wild friends. If your parents are bad, make them sit in their room and do your homework. Make sure you supervise what your parents are wearing at all times. Don't let your parents have any treats before supper.

Renee Hagins, 8th Grade
North Brunswick, New Jersey

Practical Matters

Bedtime

Parents should let children go to bed when they want.

Amanda Kent, 3rd Grade
Hampstead, Maryland

I wish I could not have to go to bed so early. Even though if you go to bed early you most likely get more sleep.

Julie R. Stone, 5th Grade
Spartanburg, South Carolina

I wish I could go to bed at 1:59 A.M. because I do not like to go to bed early. I go to bed at 9:05 or earlier. I am glad I do not have to go to bed at 5:00 in the afternoon.

Tiffanee Westland, 3rd Grade
Northridge, California

Parents should let children go to bed whenever they want to, up to about eleven o'clock, without a lifetime story (how they went to bed at six and woke with the roosters and walked on that weary journey to school—after they made the bread for their toast—uphill both ways).

John Lambe, 5th Grade
Canton, Michigan

Bedtime for Parents?

I wish my parents would go to bed before me.

Laura S. Piskoz, 1st Grade
Hurley, New York

They should have a certain time to go to bed so that they won't be grumpy the next day, and so they'll get up the next morning.

Troy Ramey, 5th Grade
Mitchell, Indiana

Chores

The parents should clean up their own messes. They think we're just little maids.

Tina Barnes, 8th Grade
Charleston, Illinois

If the child's room is a mess but if he knows where everything is he should be able to keep it that way.

Josh Ebert, 6th Grade
Apple Creek, Ohio

They always yell at me for leaving my stuff laying around when their stuff is all over the place too.

John Oslin, 8th Grade
Hartland, Michigan

I will mak them do the dishis and clen the hol hows and I jost sit and relaks.

Ty James Eitel, 2nd Grade
Latimer, Iowa

13

Mothers should not ask their daughters to do house-work. They are going to do it when they get older anyway. If a mother resents housework, then why did she get married!!!

Laurie Paul, 8th Grade
North Brunswick, New Jersey

Rake your own lawn, you bought it.

Christopher Lum, 6th Grade
Palo Alto, California

Don't make your bed every morning since you're just going to get back in that night.

Suzanne Yancey, 9th Grade
Graham, Texas

One rule for moms is to wash our close sooner and not lose them.

Laura Neff, age 10
San Jose, California

And While We're on the Subject

Once when I was little I warshed the car with an SOS pad and my Dad yeld at me.

Reni Piperata, 3rd Grade
Stewartsville, New Jersey

Clothes and Grooming

Did you ever notice how parents always seem to have the exact opposite taste in clothes and music than their kids have? That really bothers me. If I am going to be wearing the clothes, I should pick them out and decide whether or not it is "suitable attire for a young lady."

Sipi Bhandari, 8th Grade
North Brunswick, New Jersey

The world isn't gonna stay the same just because parents want it to.

Lynn Hooper, 9th Grade
Graham, Texas

I think it's embarrassing when your Mom makes you wear bell-bottom pants because they sway back and forth when you walk.

Brian Montgomery, 6th Grade
Frederick, Maryland

Baths: only if nessasarry.

Suzy Lemanek, 5th Grade
Canton, Michigan

Let's make *them* wear clothes that went out of style twenty years ago, just because *we* think it looks nice. Or how about giving our parents haircuts that make them look like a bum (and it's half price too).

Brian Anton, 8th Grade
Topsham, Maine

Parents should not get mad when our new clothes get ripped.

Brandon M. Brooks
Wiesbaden American Middle School
Wiesbaden, West Germany

I don't think my parents should make me wear a sweater when they are cold.

Miriam Waddell, 8th Grade
Spartanburg, South Carolina

Parents should always let their children (boy or girl) have as many holes in their ears as they want.

Melyssa Marich, 8th Grade
North Brunswick, New Jersey

Differences of Opinion, Clashes of Will

Not think that they're always right, because a lot of the time the kids are right but the parents will not admit it.

> Jeff Bryan, 8th Grade
> Bellefonte, Pennsylvania

Do not force a child to do anything against his will. This will anger the child and the results could be astounding.

> Scott Brooks, 9th Grade
> Knoxville, Tennessee

They should pay more attention to us. Like when they have company and they're talking about something and they say the wrong answer and we know the right one, they always argue with us. And of course we give in.

> Kelley Vermoch, 6th Grade
> Burr Ridge, Illinois

Keep it to yourself if I think it's neat and you don't.

> Libby Taggart, 6th Grade
> West Des Moines, Iowa

Parents and children should compromise with each other. Not compromising leads to significant arguments. This is what causes kids to become rebellious. In losing your cool, things can change from a mature point of view to a violent matter.

Anonymous
Boise, Idaho

Divorce and Separation

Please if you get married stay married.

Robby Melick, 4th Grade
Coopersburg, Pennsylvania

Tell the child that you and your husband haven't been getting along. Then get to the point slowly and carefully.

Adrian Kulp, 4th Grade
Coopersburg, Pennsylvania

If the parent remarries, he or she should talk to the child.

Tricia M. Battin
Wiesbaden American Middle School
Wiesbaden, West Germany

If one of your parents gets married again, don't let them leave you out.

Rebecca Skrzat, 4th Grade
Coopersburg, Pennsylvania

Often Repeated

Divorced parents shouldn't say bad things about the other parent in front of the child.

21

Don't Treat Us Like Kids!!

Don't treat them like babies unless they are babies.

> Gary Toriello, Chris Patti, 6th Grade
> West Orange, New Jersey

Parents should let their kids make their own decisions, except very serious ones.

> Lara Catherine Hansen, 6th Grade
> Matthews, North Carolina

I don't like it when my mom talks to me like I'm a stupid little kid. I'm not a little kid anymore and she stupider than I am.

> Kristen Jackson, 8th Grade
> Charleston, Illinois

You should understand we're about five years older than you treat us.

> Kara J. Bartelt, 6th Grade
> West Des Moines, Iowa

If she is over nine, do not buy her Smurf bedsheets, Underoos, or strawberry shortcake bubble bath.

> Sally Rosenthal, 6th Grade
> Sharon, Massachusetts

Don't come looking for me when I'm only five minutes late . . . No "isn't-she-sweet-going-to-her-first-
party" looks when my friends are over.

Elizabeth Grainger, 6th Grade
Montclair, California

Drinking and Drugs

Parents should not drink because it can give us kids a bad repretation.

> Robin A. Long, 6th Grade
> McAlester, Oklahoma

Don't take drugs like beer.

> Stephanie Parks, 2nd Grade
> Fort Worth, Texas

I think parents shouldn't let kids even look at drugs.

> Brian Orr, 6th Grade
> Apple Creek, Ohio

Parents should never do drugs with their children.

> Wes Tragesser, 9th Grade
> Wabash, Indiana

I would take him or her to the nut floor of the hospital to see all the people that's in there from taking drugs.

> James Deric Pappan, 8th Grade
> Ponca City, Oklahoma

Encouragement and Love

When I give you a hug, give me two hugs back.

Michael Reinberger, 1st Grade
Antioch, California

I have never had anyone tell me they love me, my parents weren't the loving type, I would do anything to get my parents to show a little love.

Anonymous, 9th Grade
Wabash, Indiana

Don't get upset if we don't do nothing right.

Deloris Paula Hornbeck, 7th Grade
Reader, West Virginia

Many times in life a kid will not make a team or some other kind of activity and will feel like a total reject. That's when a parent should say, "Hey, it's OK, you did your best and that's what counts."

Esther Hanscom, 9th Grade
Machias, Maine

Etiquette

Manners makes a good parent.

> Quincy Manning
> Greensboro, North Carolina

I think parents should be polite. They talk when they eat. They talk when I am. They always do that.

> Rodney Lee, Jr.; 2nd Grade
> Bellefonte, Pennsylvania

I think we should be able to put our arm on the table when we eat.

> Ron Carlson
> Greensburg, Ohio

Make parents close their mouth when they chew.

> Michael B. Kinlaw, 6th Grade
> Altavista, Virginia

Family Activities
and Time Together

Parents can give things to their children or they can spend time with their children. Time is best.

Matthew Addison, 3rd Grade
Nederland, Texas

Kids are very sensitive. The parents can maybe spend time with your child to get really close, cause I'm a kid myself and when my mom spends time with me I feel like I'm the most specialist kid in the world and she feels the same way.

Staci Sickles, 6th Grade
West Orange, New Jersey

You should do things with your kids a lot of the time. My parents didn't do very much with me, and I always had to find something to do on my own. That's probably most of the reason why I'm here. *

Anonymous, 9th Grade
Wabash, Indiana

Play with us for ten minutes everyday.

Jake Stingle, 2nd Grade
Clearwater, Florida

* In a residential school for juveniles in trouble with the law.

Parents should let the child in on some of their conversations.

Tricia M. Battin
Wiesbaden American Middle School
Wiesbaden, West Germany

Please go to bed with me.

Larry DeCamillo, 1st Grade
Hawthorne, New York

Fights

Parents should not interfere in children's pillow fights, if they don't want to be hit by a flying pillow.

Bruce Milligan, 3rd Grade
Darien, Connecticut

You may only blame somebody if you saw the incident.

Kevin Scott, 5th Grade
Aurora, Colorado

Whenever there is a fight between two of your children, take the side of the one with the most dramatic production.

Mary Rank, 5th Grade
Downers Grove, Illinois

Parents should remember during fights that their children are always right.

Susan Sattan, 8th Grade
North Brunswick, New Jersey

Your children may just be letting off steam by doing something horrid. They are not making a personal insult to you.

Lisa Giles, 8th Grade
Topsham, Maine

31

Make notes of everything they say so later on they don't say something like, "I never told you that!" when you know they did.

Kimberly Phillips, 8th Grade
Escondido, California

Food

Lobster every Wednesday with shrimp and steamed clams.

K. Grant Way
Boiceville, New York

Parents are always saying, "Eat all your greens." This should include green candy, too.

Bruce Milligan, 3rd Grade
Darien, Connecticut

Make sure your child eats the right foods. Junk foods can really trick you. They are really packed with vitamins and bursting with nutrients.

Kristen Mitchell, 6th Grade
Herndon, Virginia

I don't like eggplant or lemon meringue pies. I don't like tomatoes fried and I don't care for lamb chops and that's all I have to say.

Jesse Carlson, 4th Grade
Oakland, California

Do not make me eat tofu and white cauliflower.

Nathan Collins
Boiceville, New York

I'd like to get a Penguin's Frozen Yogurt every day and get to go to Chuck E. Cheese whenever I wanted.

Vanessa Voss, 3rd Grade
Northridge, California

They can't lick the cake mix bowl.

Rita M. Flaherty, 6th Grade
Syracuse, New York

Don't talk too long when you are cooking, the food might burn.

J. Craig Williams, Jr., 2nd Grade
Clearwater, Florida

You may not force-feed your children.

Kristin Toft, 6th Grade
West Des Moines, Iowa

Cook more good stuff.

Paul Trost, 4th Grade
Alief, Texas

One Final Plea

I wish my mom would cook a little better.

Ken Dupcak, 3rd Grade
Northridge, California

Friends, Dating, and Sex

Thou shalt not pick at thy child because of their out-
landish friends.

> Rachael Wharton and Susan Danewitz, 6th Grade
> Herndon, Virginia

Never take your teenager anywhere where there will
not be another teenager.

> Jennifer Turner, 8th Grade
> Spartanburg, South Carolina

When they go to parties don't ask who was there,
how many people were there, were there any boys
there, who were they, what did you do, did you eat,
was the food good, did you watch a movie, what did
you watch, did you play any games, what did you play.

> Ann Moore, 9th Grade
> Graham, Texas

If your daughter brings home a boyfriend named
Moose, say nothing to her at the time, as Moose will
probably crush you.

> David Engledow, 8th Grade
> Prairie Lea, Texas

Parents must stay in their room when we have company.

> Renesha Yolanda Holmes, 6th Grade
> Bronx, New York

Parents should try to understand the way the world is today. Clothes are different, music is different, and attitudes are different. Everything is *not* the same as it was when they were kids . . . Parents should realize that children are more aware about sex than they were at that age. R-rated movies will *not* corrupt teenagers. They've probably already seen it anyway.

> Margaret Kane, 8th Grade
> North Brunswick, New Jersey

Should let boyfriend and girlfriend do what they want, to an extent.

> Brian Stone, Scott Souders, 9th Grade
> Middletown, Pennsylvania

If they have questions about sex tell them, but don't show them how to do it.

> T. J. Patton, 8th Grade
> Ponca City, Oklahoma

Why can't you have sex at school?

> Bruce Mendez, 9th Grade
> Asheville, North Carolina

If your daughter has that certain smirk on her face, don't just think about it, start to worry.

> Natalie M. Wilhelmson, 9th Grade
> Redding, California

Get me a wife.

> Nathan Pralle, 2nd Grade
> Latimer, Iowa

I Wish . . .

Parents should give us the big room. We got more things than they do.

Shellie Heskett, 6th Grade
McAlester, Oklahoma

Any idiosyncrasies or habits of the parents are subject to any jokes conceived by the children without punishments to the children.

Keith Miller, 9th Grade
Middletown, Pennsylvania

I think teenagers should have at least three to four hours to be alone because the young adolescent mind has a lot of thoughts and conclusions going through it. If a thought is cramped, the conclusion might not be the right one.

Andrew Wood, 9th Grade
Machias, Maine

Let us use your stuff.

Joleen Littlejohn, 3rd Grade
Midland, Michigan

One more thing I wish is that my parents and brother and sister would not die.

Dawn Campbell, 3rd Grade
Northridge, California

Lessons

Parents should not pressure kids into playing a dumb instrument like a bassoon.

Marc Fioravanti, 8th Grade
North Brunswick, New Jersey

Money and Other Nice Things

Money! Bring on the money!

Ana Manning, 4th Grade
Oakland, California

If children have their own money saved up, parents should let them use it for whatever they want.

Lara Hansen, 6th Grade
Matthews, North Carolina

Children should receive 50 percent of all things wanted for Christmas. (To Children: ask for 200 percent. This way you get 100 percent of everything you wanted.)

Damon Owen, 7th Grade
Solana Beach, California

Show your child you love them. An effective way is stretching their allowance. Remember, an extra dollar is an extra hug.

Kristen Mitchell, 6th Grade
Herndon, Virginia

Give to poor (like me).

Erik Anderson, 6th Grade
Pelham, New York

Don't be such tightwads.

Craig Duehlmeier, 8th Grade
Fall Creek, Wisconsin

Don't buy me an educational science kit.
Buy what I prefer or I'll throw a fit.

Tara Golden
East Brunswick, New Jersey

Please get me a waterbed.

Michael Scheringer
Boiceville, New York

Nice Try

If I was good I would get anything I want but if I was bad I would still get things but not really what I wanted.

Amy Hite, 3rd Grade
Northridge, California

The Minority View

Don't give children everything they want. Because some little toyes loock really neet but they are junck.

John A. Macari, 1st Grade
Atascadero, California

Nagging and Lectures

Parents shouldn't nag. It makes me go in my room and turn the radio up high.

> Christine Schultz, 7th Grade
> Staten Island, New York

Parents can't bore us by saying the same things over and over.

> Anthony Billotti, 6th Grade
> Deer Park, New York

Thou shalt not nag thy children about homework or school projects. When thy child gets an "A –" thou shalt not ask, "Why the minus?" Thou shalt not nag children about practicing the piano. Thou shalt not be an all-around pest.

> Martha G. Fay, 6th Grade
> Herndon, Virginia

Often Repeated

Parents always make you feel guilty—even when you don't know what they're talking about.

Pets

Don't let the dog eat on the table when we're eating.

Ashton Smith
Boiceville, New York

Do not let your child give the dog a mohawk.

David Engledow, 8th Grade
Prairie Lea, Texas

Don't let your child play with black and white cats.
They might be skunks.

Sam Dougherty, 3rd Grade
Hampstead, Maryland

Privacy and Dignity

Living with parents is like living in prison. We can't do anything without you knowing it.

> Jamie Collins, 8th Grade
> Willow Springs, Missouri

Parents, it's the kid's room, not yours. You parents always put things where we can't find them. So parents leave our rooms *alone.*

> Johanna Kleimola, 6th Grade
> Frederick, Maryland

Parents can be so nosy! My parents read *all,* I'm telling you, *all* my letters!

> Kris Moorhead, 8th Grade
> Willow Springs, Missouri

Parents are forever spying on their children. Moms and dads should step back a bit to let kids have room to grow. After all, kids don't like to have people following them around like F.B.I. agents.

> Jenny Rucker, 8th Grade
> Highland, Michigan

You stay far away when friends are over.

> Kara J. Bartelt, 6th Grade
> West Des Moines, Iowa

When a girl invites her boyfriend to dinner, absolutely do not show boyfriend baby pictures of her, especially if she is unclothed. When boyfriend comes to pick up girl, do not call him "Son" and ask his plans for the future.

Sally Rosenthal, 6th Grade
Sharon, Massachusetts

Never tease us in front of friends.

Kara J. Bartelt, 6th Grade
West Des Moines, Iowa

Do not yell at me in front of company.

Christina Martinez, 6th Grade
Montclair, California

Parents should understand when kids are in bad moods, and not ask, "How was your day at school?" when you come in the house and kick your dog and brother and sister.

Kelly Nesbitt, 8th Grade
Highland, Michigan

My mom should not clean up the closet because she throws away the good stuff.

Michele Trent, 1st Grade
Turlock, California

Never touch your teenager in public. Never say, "Oh, you've grown so much!" to any of your children's friends.

John David Vaughn, 8th Grade
Spartanburg, South Carolina

Please don't tell my friends that once I wet the bed just before a camping trip. Under no circumstances will you bring out old baby pictures.

Elizabeth Grainger, 6th Grade
Montclair, California

Don't call your daughter nicknames (such as Lambie Pie, Pumpikins, etc.) in front of friends or in public.

Sally Rosenthal, 6th Grade
Sharon, Massachusetts

Don't ask stupid questions in front of her friends. "What is heavy metal?" or "Who's Eddie Murphy?" are examples of how out-of-it parents are. Chill out, and ask her later.

Cecelia Collins, 9th Grade
Middletown, Pennsylvania

NEVER ask your child to play her instrument for your friends.

Anne Lin, 6th Grade
Sharon, Massachusetts

When talking on the phone to a neighbor about your teenager, don't say, "I could hardly keep my face straight when he/she was telling me about it," or "Isn't that cute?"

Sheila Dunleavy, 8th Grade
Hartland, Michigan

Punishment, Discipline, and Yelling

If a kid lies I think your parents should let God take care of it.

David A. Wheeler, 4th Grade
Coopersburg, Pennsylvania

When a child commits a punishable act, tell him to punish himself.

Scott Brooks, 9th Grade
Knoxville, Tennessee

If you punish a child for doing something wrong, it is wrong, because every body does something wrong in their life.

Melissa Bissinger, 4th Grade
Coopersburg, Pennsylvania

I think children should be punished but not too pun-ished.

Kathryn Lin, 6th Grade
Palo Alto, California

My parents should not slap my mouth because I don't want to lose any more teeth.

Christopher Dove, 2nd Grade
Cleona, Pennsylvania

Parents should not beat on us because they love us so much.

Victoria Apodaca, 6th Grade
Glendale, Arizona

When you have a whiner for a daughter you must learn to restrict her howling. Just grab her backside and give a few swats . . . just enough to remember.

Michelle M. DeWitte, 8th Grade
Highland, Michigan

Don't tell us to stop yelling by yelling.

Megan Reynolds, 6th Grade
Yonkers, New York

When my dad or mom yells at me I don't listen like I would if they just talked to me.

John Oslin, 8th Grade
Hartland, Michigan

Parents shouldn't continue yelling about things that happened weeks ago.

Shannon Teter, 7th Grade
Yonkers, New York

Kids should be punished but not till parents are sure us kids did it.

Jennifer Adams, 6th Grade
McAlester, Oklahoma

Do not punish us if you also break the same rule.

Gregory Davis, 5th Grade
Pelham, New York

Let *me* ground *you* when *you* fight.

Kimberly Rougeux
Boiceville, New York

"Go to your room"? What is the point of going to your room—the place where the average teen spends half their life in, with most of the essentials they need or want—when they get in trouble? If your parents want to punish you, why don't they make you sit with them downstairs?

Lori Bobroy, 8th Grade
North Brunswick, New Jersey

If they spill juice don't hit them in the hiny while cleaning it.

Joe Davila, 6th Grade
West Orange, New Jersey

A lot of times we get into trouble for things we didn't even do. Then when they find out the truth, their ego is so big they can't even apologize.

Jamie K. Austin, 6th Grade
Hudson, Michigan

Don't take advice from other parents about punishment.

Melissa Griffin, 6th Grade
Raleigh, North Carolina

Don't let your teenagers take over the house, because you will have a hard time getting it back.

Riggan Acosta, 8th Grade
Prairie Lea, Texas

If I obeyed every guideline my parents set, I would be bored to death.

Sally Nichols, 8th Grade
Willow Springs, Missouri

Never tell your teenager to take the dog for a walk when you get mad at them.

Jennifer Turner, 8th Grade
Spartanburg, South Carolina

There's nothing more frustrating for a kid than being punished without having a chance to explain.

Serena Foulke, 8th Grade
Escondido, California

When I do something wrong my Mom and Dad shouldn't ground me. They should talk to me or smack me and get it over with. When I'm grounded it seems like five thousand years.

Glenn Reiss, 4th Grade
Coopersburg, Pennsylvania

Religion and Ethics

If the parents are Christians they should not push religion on their kids. If the kid wants to be a Christian he/she will. But it should be up to the kid, not the parent.

> Lisa Renner, 9th Grade
> Wabash, Indiana

Don't try to force your values and beliefs on the children when they get older.

> Kenneth McKnight, 7th Grade
> Flint, Michigan

Parents should obey God. Parents should not obey Satan.

> Karin Y. Davis, 4th Grade
> Dearing, Georgia

School and Homework

Let kids stay home from school on Jewish holidays when they're not Jewish.

Mark Mayhew, 6th Grade
Matthews, North Carolina

One time I got two C's. My father wasn't too happy. But one day my mom had out a box of junk and we found my dad's report cards. He wasn't too great either.

Brandon Howard, 6th Grade
Indianola, Iowa

Parents should try to understand if they find a test or paper in the trash with an "F". After all, how often did they show their parents a paper with an "F"?

Shannon Teter, 7th Grade
Yonkers, New York

I really hate it when I get a bad grade and get chewed out for it. My mom tells me she doesn't care about my grades as long as I do my best, then all of a sudden she's yelling because of a bad grade.

Chad Burrow, 6th Grade
McAlester, Oklahoma

Siblings

Parents shouldn't like one child more than the other.

> Marcus Nelson, 4th Grade
> Mattoon, Illinois

You shouldn't yell at the older kid for everything.

> Kristin Randall, 5th Grade
> Canton, Michigan

If big brothers or sisters pick on you, parents must fire them from family.

> Kevin Lovato, 7th Grade
> Glendale, Arizona

Kill my sister. No, I'm just kidding.

> Patty Lee, 5th Grade
> Spartanburg, South Carolina

Parents should not let our big brothers or sisters beat up on us.

> Dawn Alex, 5th Grade
> Canton, Michigan

Sell my brother for a dog of my own.

Laura Blanks, 6th Grade
Altavista, Virginia

Parents shouldn't make young kids obey their older brothers and sisters.

Leslie Neide, 4th Grade
National Park, New Jersey

Parents should have only one child. This would make less population, no sibling rivalry, shorter Christmas shopping lists, and more money for everyone.

Anissa Mihalek, 8th Grade
Hartland, Michigan

I think my parents are great. They raised me great. I wish they didn't raise my sister.

Ryan Johnson, 6th Grade
Auburn, Washington

Talking Things Over

Give me a better answer than "because I said so."

Kumrob Singtoe Maungyoo
Boiceville, New York

Parents should listen more to their kids. It seems like when we talk there's always something on TV or they just act spaced out to make you believe they're listening but when you ask them a question they say I was listening to the TV, will you repeat it?

Rondell Prewitt
Wiesbaden American Middle School
Wiesbaden, West Germany

Listen to the unimportant things so they'll tell you the important things.

Tara Peterson, 7th Grade
Escondido, California

Let us finish what we're saying instead of cutting us off and saying, "NO WAY!"

Heather Byrd, 6th Grade
Frederick, Maryland

A lot of parents have trouble talking to their children. My mom would always say, "Do what you want to do." We never had a conversation. If so, it was all screaming and yelling.

Anonymous, 9th Grade
Wabash, Indiana

Telephone

Don't stay on the phone too long because your ear might fall off.

Vincent A. Guido, 2nd Grade
Cleona, Pennsylvania

Never tell your teenager to get off the phone. If they talk to their friends at night, they won't talk to them in school.

Jennifer Turner, 8th Grade
Spartanburg, South Carolina

Trust, Responsibilities, and Freedom: Room to Grow

I wish they'd put more trust in me. I know I probably used up most of it before, but I really think I've changed.

Lynn McKinnie, 8th Grade
Escondido, California

They shouldn't jump to conclusions like they sometimes do.

Julia R. Grimes, 6th Grade
Apple Creek, Ohio

If you trust them and let them do what they want maybe they wouldn't be so bad.

Dawna Marie Bares, 6th Grade
Auburn, Washington

There's a difference between protective and overprotective! When parents are overprotective, the child or children often start lying about where they are and what they're doing. Then, the parents are putting their children in more danger.

Jill Board, 8th Grade
Charleston, Illinois

They say I have to learn from experience, but if they don't let me do anything, how am I supposed to learn?

Leslie Beckham, 9th Grade
Graham, Texas

TV, Movies, Music

Set a good example for your children! Watching TV is a very good example.

> Kristen Mitchell, 6th Grade
> Herndon, Virginia

No watching sapoperas and women shows.

> Elizabeth Trainor, 4th Grade
> Oyster Bay, New York

If my parents are watching the news and I can't talk loud then they should have to whisper when I'm watching my TV shows.

> Angela Ravan, 5th Grade
> Spartanburg, South Carolina

My Dad says I have to be quiet when we're watching TV and when I'm watching TV he won't be quiet and I don't like it. I wish he would be quiet. I wish I had a solution.

> Tina Hughes, 4th Grade
> Indianapolis, Indiana

Why can't I see dirty movies?

> Gus Schnitzer
> Boiceville, New York

Remember, parents, that Motley Crue and Madonna are today what Elvis, the Beatles, and the Rolling Stones were yesterday.

Tadd Sholtis, 9th Grade
Middletown, Pennsylvania

Quit hiding my Madonna tape.

Michael Berti
Boiceville, New York

Other Issues

Behavior Modification for Parents

Fathers: Never wear navy socks with shorts.

> John David Vaughn, 8th Grade
> Spartanburg, South Carolina

Don't wear dorky clothes.

> Michelle Mack, 8th Grade
> Fall Creek, Wisconsin

They should learn to act cool with your friends, for example, like if I brought my friend home I wouldn't want my Mom to act stupid.

> DeeDee Susen, 8th Grade
> Fall Creek, Wisconsin

Parents' clothes shouldn't clash.

> Kim Crandall, 8th Grade
> Fall Creek, Wisconsin

Parents should stop saying they're on diets while they're eating junk food.

> Peter Ioveno, 6th Grade
> Deer Park, New York

Wear hip clothes in public, don't wear ugly things like flowered muumuus and orange-and-green-checked polyester pants suits.

> Sally Rosenthal, 6th Grade
> Sharon, Massachusetts

I think parents should laugh.

> Cristin Hutchinson
> Barstow, California

Parents shouldn't fall asleep on the couch. You want to watch a movie and you can't find a good spot on the couch. If they're that tired I think they should go to bed. I also think they should go to bed early're than they are because my mom can't cook in the morning and my dad can't get to work on time.

> Jeffrey Bobbett, 4th Grade
> Skaneateles, New York

If you gripe and grumble all the time, what do you expect your children to do? If you are positive, they will have a more positive attitude.

> Tammy Hoyer, 8th Grade
> Superior, Nebraska

Never make your child feel embarrassed; therefore, never sing in public.

> Anne Lin, 6th Grade
> Sharon, Massachusetts

Don't say bad words at football games. You will wake up the baby.

> Joseph Taylor, 2nd Grade
> Neptune, New Jersey

Parents should *never* tell their kids, "We never did that when we were young," because they probably did.

Jeff Wright and Scott Syke, 8th Grade
Highland, Michigan

No hand-holding in public places.

Wendi Joy Bethel, 9th Grade
Knoxville, Tennessee

No kissing until bedtime.

Brian E. Higgins, 7th Grade
Reader, West Virginia

Help others in the family or society when they need help.

Larry E. Wildey, Jr., 6th Grade
Richmond, Indiana

Don't try so hard to be perfect. Parents don't seem to understand that kids know when their mom or dad has had a bad day.

Sheila Dunleavy, 8th Grade
Hartland, Michigan.

Pleas for Justice

What really bugs me is the first twelve months of a kid's life their parents are teaching them to walk and talk, and in the next twelve years they tell 'em to sit down and shut up.

Justina Myers, 5th Grade
Ephrata, Washington

Do not tell me what I can't do then you turn around and do it.

John R. Peters, 7th Grade
Reader, West Virginia

Some people think their kids have to go through it just like they had to. That is really dumb because the children didn't do anything to deserve such a hard childhood.

Shelly Johnson, 8th Grade
Escondido, California

We kids should have fun when we are at our younger ages because when we old people we can't do nothing but work all of the time, and that sure isn't fun.

Jeff King, 8th Grade
Charleston, Illinois

When a girl asks to do something the answer is usually "no," but when a boy asks the answer will most likely be "yes."

Debra Joy, 9th Grade
Machias, Maine

Everytime she goes shopping I just have to look at the ladies department, and I'm the one that gets tired of walking because she's in there for one hour or more!!!

David Mullen, 4th Grade
Carroll, Ohio

Don't throw away our toys.

Alan Asiala, 3rd Grade
Midland, Michigan

What can you expect? You've only been around for fifteen years, you're treated like you're two, you do something wrong, they tell you to act your age and be a responsible adult.

Steven C. Warren, 9th Grade
Knoxville, Tennessee

You shouldn't say, "You're responsible for losing your toys!" then later say, "Help me find my keys."

Jason George, 5th Grade
San Jose, California

Remember, kids aren't perfect and make mistakes. That's what growing up is all about.

Lynnette Huddlestun, 8th Grade
Charleston, Illinois

If you find a frog in the bathtub, don't blame your child first. It might have been your husband.

Lynda Jackson, 9th Grade
Redding, California

When your kids do something you just told them not to do, don't get mad, you probably did the same thing when you were a tyke.

Rob Stevenson, 8th Grade
Highland, Michigan

What if they were in our position and we did them like they do us sometimes?

Autumn Baughman, 5th Grade
Mitchell, Indiana

General Tips

When it rains, wear a raincoat.

Rosio Rendon, 1st Grade
Turlock, California

Don't get arrested.

Frank DiFusco, 6th Grade
Somerville, Massachusetts

Try not to catch on fire.

Zack Ring, 2nd Grade
St. Maries, Idaho

Be an example, because kids need someone to pattern themselves after, and it might as well be you.

Lisa Powers, 8th Grade
Willow Springs, Missouri

Don't be a hobo.

Nasha Y. Shaw, 2nd Grade
Clearwater, Florida

Do not ever, ever kill.

Mike Frost, 2nd Grade
St. Maries, Idaho

Don't yell at your child during their nightmares or you'll have bad results.

Andrew Rittler, 3rd Grade
Hampstead, Maryland

Don't name your child with an embarrassing name or initials (such as Zachary Ian Thompson—ZIT).

Priya Sarin and Heather Van Dyke
Fremont, California

Be carful.

Andrea Lawrence, 2nd Grade
Randallstown, Maryland

Parents should make us feel that we need parents.

Brian Pickrell, 4th Grade
Lawton, Michigan

To Be More Specific . . .

Stop signing me up for the flouride rinse at school.

> Aaron Gillum, Jeremy Trumble, Chris
> Gatti, Sarah Nevels, 3rd Grade
> Union, Kentucky

Help them find Halley's Comet.

> Sheryl R. Mitchell
> Altavista, Virginia

I wish that my mummy would go down to the basement and pick up all the doo doo and the feathers from our pigeons.

> Carly O'Keefe Grey, 1st Grade
> Hurley, New York

Please offer your bed *not mine* when company comes.

> Megan Wallace, 5th Grade
> Aurora, Colorado

Get HBO. Stay out of my room. Let me open an eagle zoo in our backyard.

> Wayne Nitzschner
> Boiceville, New York

Always wear steel-toe boots so your toes aren't broken when you kick the wall in frustration over your bundle of joy.

Kyle Hagemann, 7th Grade
Santa Rosa, California

Often Repeated

Don't make me go to Aunt ____'s.

Not So Much to Ask

Love me if you have time.

> Laura Blanks, 6th Grade
> Altavista, Virginia

Don't make me talk to company (unless I want).

> Debra Barr, age 11
> Rosston, Arkansas

They also must let me have a birthday every year.

> Kathy Hules, 7th Grade
> Glendale, Arizona

Please let me go to Laura's house.

> Jimmy Harrison, 1st Grade
> Hawthorne, New York

Say What?

If a child gets hit by a high school, say pick on someone your own size.

Allison Abbot, 4th Grade
Conneautville, Pennsylvania

Hair: if child likes it.

Suzy Lemanek, 5th Grade
Canton, Michigan

Remember, these are the 80s, not the 60s. Kids are
more dependent now.

John Rossi, 6th Grade
West Des Moines, Iowa

Mothers should make sure you washed yourself and
most of all your ears, because they might just stand in
the tub. See what I mean?

Dan Schramek, 3rd Grade
Holland, Pennsylvania

Show your child that people in other countries can be
trusted even if they are involved in military actions.

Tony Feller, 8th Grade
Richmond, Indiana

Serious Requests

Parents must realize that their children are their own people, not an extension from themselves.

Sandy O'Donnell, 8th Grade
Hartland, Michigan

Parents should try being a kid's friend instead of a parent.

Kim Owens, 8th Grade
Willow Springs, Missouri

Love your kids enough to let them hate you.

Jennifer Austin, 5th Grade
Puyallup, Washington

If you have experienced an unfortunate past, try not to repeat history and avoid making the mistakes your parents have.

Anonymous
Boise, Idaho

Leave us alone for four or five hours a week, to give us time to become free of everything.

Suzie F. Cox, 8th Grade
Hartland, Michigan

Another rule would be that they should take my opinion into consideration when making decisions that affect me. Or take my solutions, ideas, and thoughts seriously.

Cristin Carley, 6th Grade
Pelham, New York

When the child makes sense, do not refer to him as a smart-aleck.

Anonymous
Boise, Idaho

Parents shouldn't judge their children by someone else's child.

Michele Myers, 8th Grade
Willow Springs, Missouri

Being a teenager is a very painful experience, even though many find it hard to believe. Try to think back on the times when you were a teenager. Everything happens in the teenage years: pimples, nasty teachers, hopeless crushes, bad grades in school—a tug of war between friends and family, and more pimples.

Sarah Polle, 8th Grade
Pullman, Washington

I think that parents should let their children have fun. After all, your school years will end sooner or later and if you don't get to have a good time you won't have anything to look back at.

Raymond Moore, 8th Grade
Willow Springs, Missouri

First be sure you want to be a parent.

Karen Jasper, 8th Grade
Bellefonte, Pennsylvania

YOU BE THE BOSS—but be a nice one!

Aaron Gillum, Jeremy Trumble, Chris
Gatti, Sarah Nevels, 3rd Grade
Union, Kentucky

Often Repeated

Don't touch children where they don't want to be
touched.

In Conclusion,
Let Me Just Say . . .

Parents should be nice to their children because they'll be their children forever.

> Stephanie Haynes, 4th Grade
> Branford, Connecticut

Spend lots of time with them and enjoy them because they grow up fast.

> Jason Teick, 5th Grade
> Redwood Falls, Minnesota

My advice to parents is to go easy on your children, because they will take care of you later on in your life.

> Brian A. Molde, 8th Grade
> Charleston, Illinois

If none of that works, there's one thing you can do— go to your room, shut the door and HAVE A NEVIS BREAKDOWN!

> Jeff Hunter, 3rd Grade
> Holland, Pennsylvania

If that doesn't work, write to Dear Abby.

Justin Bliffen, 3rd Grade
Holland, Pennsylvania

Thank you for reading this and doing what I wrote I hope.

Heather Andrews, 4th Grade
Indianapolis, Indiana

I really wish all these things. But I don't think they will all come true.

Caroline Kim, 3rd Grade
Northridge, California

Don't forget to turn your parents off at night.

Daniel E. Eldred, 8th Grade
Highland, Michigan

Or, on the Other Hand

I would'n have kids to begin with.

Jeremy Strouse, 8th Grade
Bellefonte, Pennsylvania

Acknowledgments

Our thanks to the editors who ran our notices, and to the teachers' magazines themselves: Ann Kurzius at *NEA Today* and Patricia Broderick at *Early Years*.

To the teachers we owe our greatest debt of gratitude. Not only did they assign our topic to their classes, but their sensitive discussions triggered tremendous outpourings of creative and thoughtful writing. Here then, by state and city, is a list of the teachers who contributed to this book:

Arizona

Glendale: Julie Viering, 5th, 6th, and 7th Grades, St. Louis the King School

Arkansas

Rosston: Beth McAteer, 5th and 6th Grades, Bodcaw School

California

Antioch: Ginny Trownsue, 1st Grade, Marsh School
Atascadero: Jeannine McCullagh, 1st and 2nd Grades, Monterey Road Elementary School
Barstow: Kay Milender, 1st and 2nd Grades, Skyline North Elementary School
Escondido: Samye Hill, 8th Grade, Grant Junior High School
Fremont: Kris Gialdini, Warwick School
Los Gatos: Glenis Zuhlke, 5th Grade, Valley Christian School
Montclair: Sandra Barker, 6th Grade, Moreno Elementary School

Northridge: Tina Theodoratos, 3rd Grade, Saint Nicholas
School
Oakland: Judi O'Toole, 4th Grade, Carden Redwood School
Palo Alto: Renee Stapleton, 6th Grade, Hoover Elementary
School
Redding: Evlyn Hautala, 9th Grade, Nova High School
Santa Rosa: Joni Yeiter, 7th Grade, Cook Junior High School
Solana Beach: B. J. Brown, English 7th Grade, Earl Warren
Junior High School
Turlock: Sandie Sing, 1st Grade, Julien School

Colorado

Aurora: Judith Sullivan, 5th and 6th Grades, Village East
Community Elementary School
Westminster: Jill Nagrodsky, 5th Grade, Vista Grande
Elementary School

Connecticut

Branford: Susan Spear, 4th Grade, John B. Sliney School
Darien: Florence S. Temko, 3rd Grade, Ox Ridge School

Florida

Clearwater: Susan Keller, Reading Specialist; Mrs. Weber,
2nd Grade, Plumb Elementary School

Georgia

Dearing: Jan McTier, 4th Grade, Dearing Elementary School

Idaho

Boise: Sylvia Chariton, Adolescent Program, St. Alphonsus
Regional Medical Center
St. Maries: Charlotte Applegate, 2nd Grade, Heyburn
Elementary School

Illinois

Burr Ridge: Clorinda Muligano, 6th Grade, Gower Middle School

Charleston: Karen Garrett and Juanita Sherwood, 8th Grade, Charleston Junior High School

Downers Grove: Mrs. Trojanowski, 6th Grade, Pierce Downer School

Mattoon: Kathy Crawford, 4th Grade, Lincoln School

Indiana

Indianapolis: Marilyn Renner, 4th Grade

Indianapolis: Karen Roethke, 4th Grade

Mitchell: Linda Greene, 5th Grade, Burris Elementary School

Richmond: Rita Wiley, 8th Grade, Test Middle School

Wabash: Jane Hoffman, 9th Grade, White's High School

Iowa

Indianola: Ruth Kellogg, 6th Grade, Middle School

Latimer: Shirley Knudsen, 2nd Grade, CAL School

West Des Moines: Mary Burns, 6th Grade, Western Hills Elementary School

Kentucky

Union: Judith L. Hodge, 3rd Grade, New Haven Elementary School

Maine

Machias: Sherri Gould, 9th Grade, Machias Memorial High School

Topsham: Marcia Howell, 8th Grade, Mt. Ararat School

Maryland

Frederick: Laura Smith, 6th Grade, West Frederick Middle School

Hampstead: Mary Kepple, 3rd Grade, Hampstead Elementary School

Randallstown: Sheri Blum, 2nd Grade, Hernwood Elementary School

Massachusetts

Somerville: Christine Molinero, 6th Grade, Lincoln Park
Community School

Michigan

Canton: Stu Raben, 5th Grade, Field Elementary School
Flint: Mrs. H.L. Burton, 7th Grade, Whittier Middle School
Hartland: Ruth Ann Bullard, 8th Grade, Hartland Farms
Middle School
Highland: Barbara J. Rebbeck, 8th Grade, Highland Junior
High School
Hudson: John Van Havel, 6th Grade, Lincoln Elementary
Lawton: Jean Hager, 4th Grade, Mattawan Elementary School
Midland: Mary Mersereau-Kempf, 3rd Grade, Chippewassee
Elementary School

Minnesota

Redwood Falls: Gale Morley, 5th Grade, Reede Gray School

Missouri

Willow Springs: Gail Hill, 8th Grade, Willow Springs Middle
School

Nebraska

Superior: Avis Shaw, 8th Grade, Cadams School

New Jersey

National Park: Mrs. Fiedler, 4th and 5th Grades, National Park
Board of Education
Neptune: Peg Sullivan, 2nd Grade, Summerfield School
North Brunswick: Rosemarie Wiener, English and Reading,
Linwood School
Stewartsville: Virginia Schocker, 3rd Grade, Stewartsville
School
West Orange: Madeline Miller, 6th Grade, Washington School

New York

Boiceville: Constance Vanni, 5th and 6th Grades,
   R. R. Bennett Elementary School
Bronx: Mrs. Ciuffetelli, 6th Grade, Intermediate School 162
Deer Park: Miss Ryan, 6th Grade, John F. Kennedy School
Hawthorne: Mrs. Grollimund, 1st Grade, Holy Rosary School
Hurley: Elissa A. Dini, 1st Grade, Ernest C. Myer School
New Hartford: Vicki Angell, 6th Grade, E. B. Hughes
   Elementary School
Oyster Bay: Richard Siegelman, G.I.F.T.E.D. 1st–6th Grades,
   Roosevelt Elementary and Vernon Middle Schools
Pelham: Joanne Carobene, 5th Grade, and Mrs. B. Bertsch,
   6th Grade, Colonial School
Skaneateles: Miss L. Harter, 4th Grade, State Street School
Staten Island: Mary Langton, 7th Grade, Our Lady Queen of
   Peace School
Syracuse: John Price, 6th Grade English, Onondaga Hill Middle
   School
Yonkers: Linda D. Peko, Saint Mark's Evangelical Lutheran
   School

North Carolina

Asheville: Belle E. Ellebrecht, C. A. Erwin High School
Greensboro: Roberta Tann, Claxton School
Matthews: Gloria Wansley, 6th Grade, Matthews School
Raleigh: Margaret G. Sumrell, 6th Grade, Ligon Gifted and
   Talented Middle School

Ohio

Apple Creek: Mrs. Bucher, 6th Grade, Apple Creek Elementary
   School
Carroll: Richard Hilgert, 4th Grade
Greensburg: Barbara O'Connor, Kleckner Elementary School

Oklahoma

McAlester: Lisa Jones, 6th Grade, Washington School
Ponca City: Jackie Bufton, 8th Grade, West Junior High School

Pennsylvania

Bellefonte: Ruth A. Bell, 2nd Grade, Benner Elementary School

Bellefonte: William P. Fleckenstein, 8th Grade, Bellefonte Area Middle School

Cleona: Joy Hartmann, 2nd Grade, Cleona Elementary School

Conneautville: Colleen Gray, 4th Grade, Conneaut Valley Elementary

Coopersburg: Kathleen Kale, 4th Grade, Lower Milford School

Holland: Mrs. B. Ihmels, 3rd Grade, Holland Elementary School

Middletown: Janice Ford, 9th Grade, Middletown Area High School

South Carolina

Spartanburg: Edwin C. Epps, 8th Grade, McCracken Junior High School

Spartanburg: LuAnne Rogers, 5th Grade, Cannon Elementary School

Tennessee

Knoxville: Terry Runger, 9th Grade, Karns High School

Texas

Alief: Sally Harpool, 4th Grade, Youens Elementary School

Fort Worth: Mary La Wayne Hodges Hauser, 2nd Grade, West Birdville Elementary School

Graham: Carolyn G. Stroud, 9th Grade, Graham High School

Nederland: Mary Ethelyn Bosarge, 3rd Grade, Highland Park Elementary School

Prairie Lea: Denise Ronan, 8th and 9th Grades, Prairie Lea Independent School District

Virginia

Altavista: Laura D. Fortune, 6th Grade, Altavista Elementary School

Herndon: Diane Wyte, 6th Grade, Hutchison Elementary School

Washington

Auburn: Myrna Libra-Warwick, Librarian, Gildo Rey
   Elementary School
Ephrata: Mrs. D. Leichter, 5th Grade, Columbia Ridge School
Pullman: Gloria Tinder, 8th Grade, Lincoln Middle School
Puyallup: Virginia Roolf, 5th Grade

West Virginia

Reader: Linda Alexander, 7th and 8th Grades, Shortline School

Wisconsin

Fall Creek: Stephanie Fredrickson, 8th Grade, Fall Creek
   Middle School
Junction City: Terry W. Hakala, 5th and 6th Grades, Kennedy
   School

Wiesbaden, West Germany

Glenda Nall, 6th and 7th Grades, Wiesbaden American Middle
   School